D0537498

STU… …KES

Nancy Gray

Developed by the Philip Lief Group, Inc.

MICHAEL O'MARA BOOKS
LONDON

This edition published in 1993 by
Michael O'Mara Books Limited,
9 Lion Yard, Tremadoc Road,
London SW4 7NQ

Copyright © 1992 by Philip Lief
and Nancy Gray.

This edition published by arrangement
with Villard Books, a division of
Random House Inc.

Developed by the Philip Lief Group, Inc

All rights reserved. No part of this publication may be reproduced, stored in a retrieval system, or transmitted, in any form or by any means without the prior permission in writing of the publisher, nor be otherwise circulated in any form of binding or cover other than that in which it is published and without a similar condition including this condition being imposed on the subsequent purchaser.

Illustrations by Peter Maddocks

A CIP catalogue record for this book is
available from the British Library.

ISBN 1-85479-951-7

Printed and bound by Cox and Wyman,
Reading.

For Mom and Dad, who taught me the gift of laughter; and to Jeff, who keeps me sane.

ACKNOWLEDGEMENTS

Special thanks to Regina Lewis for sparking this idea; Judy Linden and Julia Banks of the Philip Lief Group, Inc., for keeping me on schedule; Creative Entertainment of Charlotte, NC, for their never-ending guidance; and to Scott and Peggy Wilson, Craig and Sally, Anna Carvalho, C. Viracola, Claudia Sherman, Robyn Feller, Carrie Carmichael, and S. Darby for their input and creativity.

INTRODUCTION

You know him, you can't avoid him, and who knows, you may even love him. Take a good look at his actions, habits, and perceptions, and you'll see what scores of women all over the country are beginning to realize: men can be the stuff of great jokes.

In the Decade of the Woman, Stupid Men Jokes are spreading faster than a middle-aged man's waistline. This raucous collection of good-natured humour certainly offers profound insight into the male of our species. It may even better your understanding of the men in your life. More than anything, it will provide hilarious respite from the war between the sexes, proving once and for all that women know a good joke when they see one.

What do you have when you have two little balls in your hand?

❦

A man's undivided attention.

What's the difference between government bonds and men?

❦

Bonds mature.

What's the difference between a man and a catfish?

❦

One's a bottom-feeding scum-sucker and the other is a fish.

What did God say after creating man?

❦

I can do better.

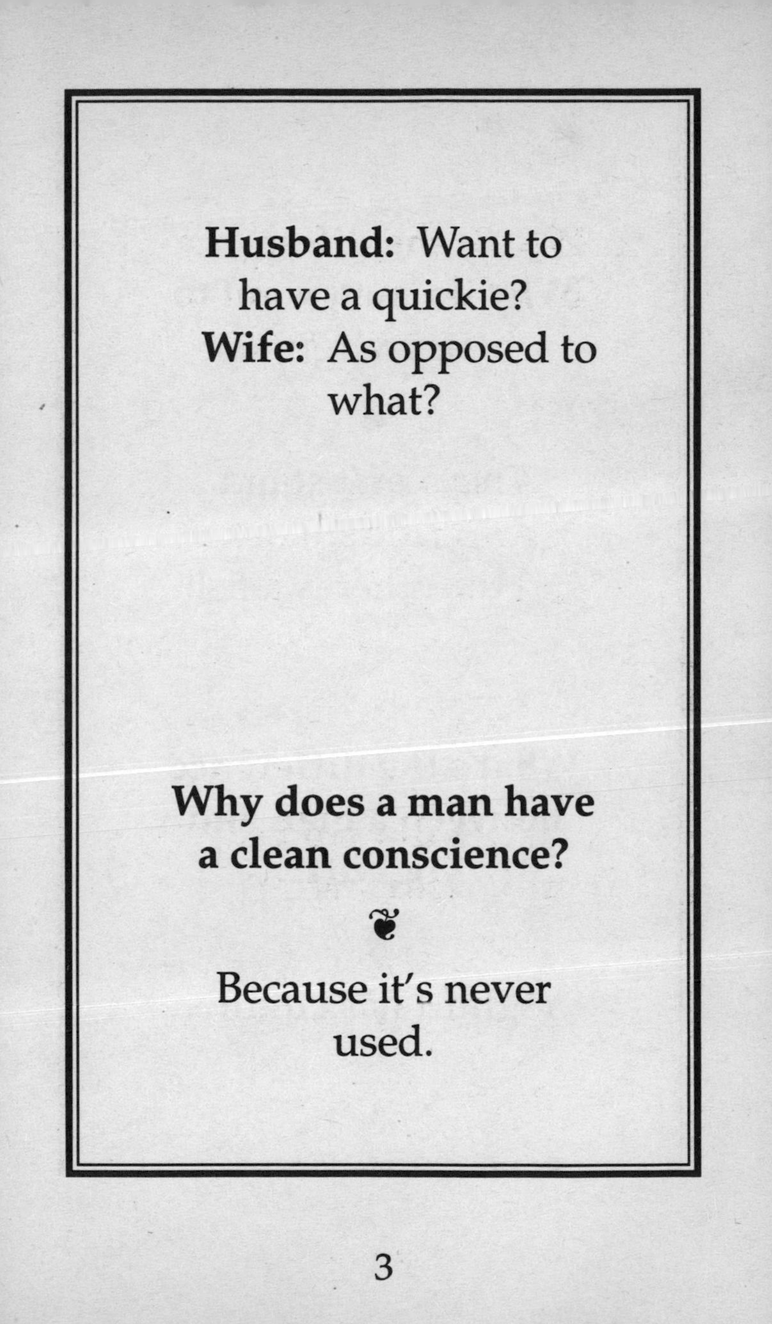

Husband: Want to have a quickie?
Wife: As opposed to what?

Why does a man have a clean conscience?

❦

Because it's never used.

Why do men want to marry virgins?

❦

They can't stand criticism.

What's the difference between a man and yoghurt?

❦

Yoghurt has culture.

Do you know what it means to come home to a man who'll give you a little time, love, and tenderness?

❦

I don't either.

What's the difference between whales and men?

❦

Whales mate for life.

Did you hear about the skier with frost-bite on his bottom?

❦

He couldn't figure out how to get his trousers over his skis.

How does a man try to calm down his nervous date their first time in bed?

❦

He simply says, "Don't worry, sweetheart, it'll just take a minute."

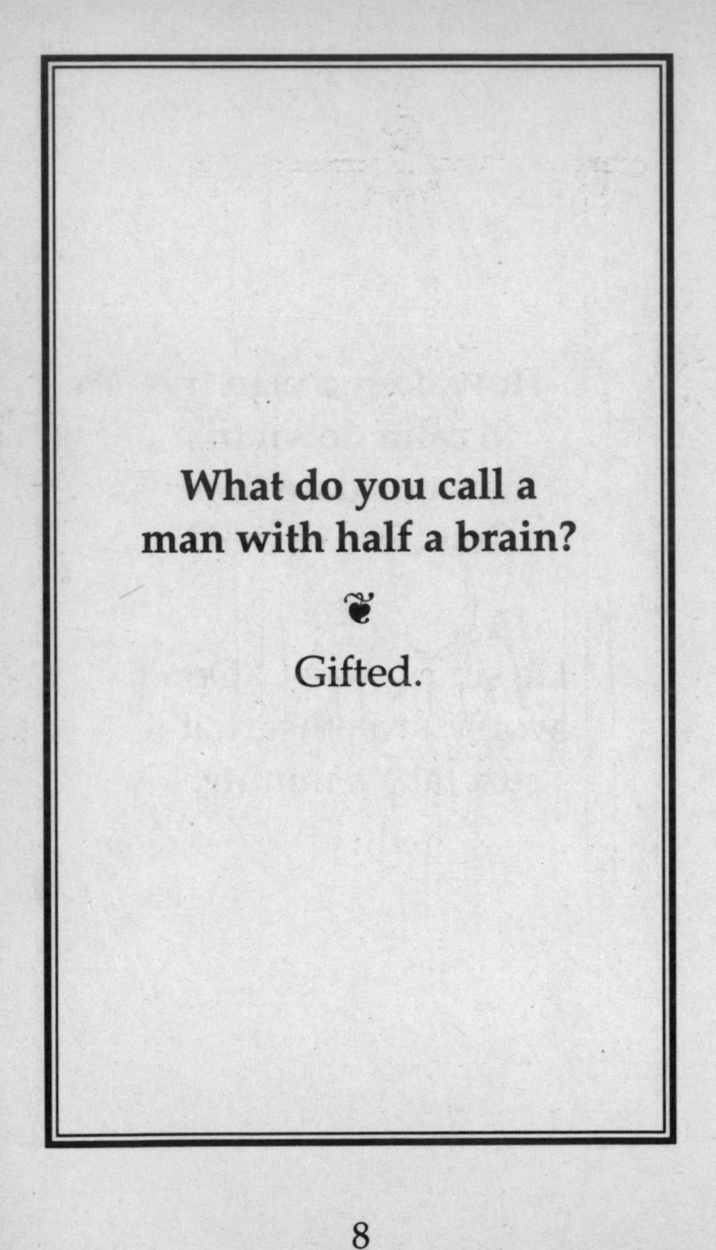

What do you call a man with half a brain?

❦

Gifted.

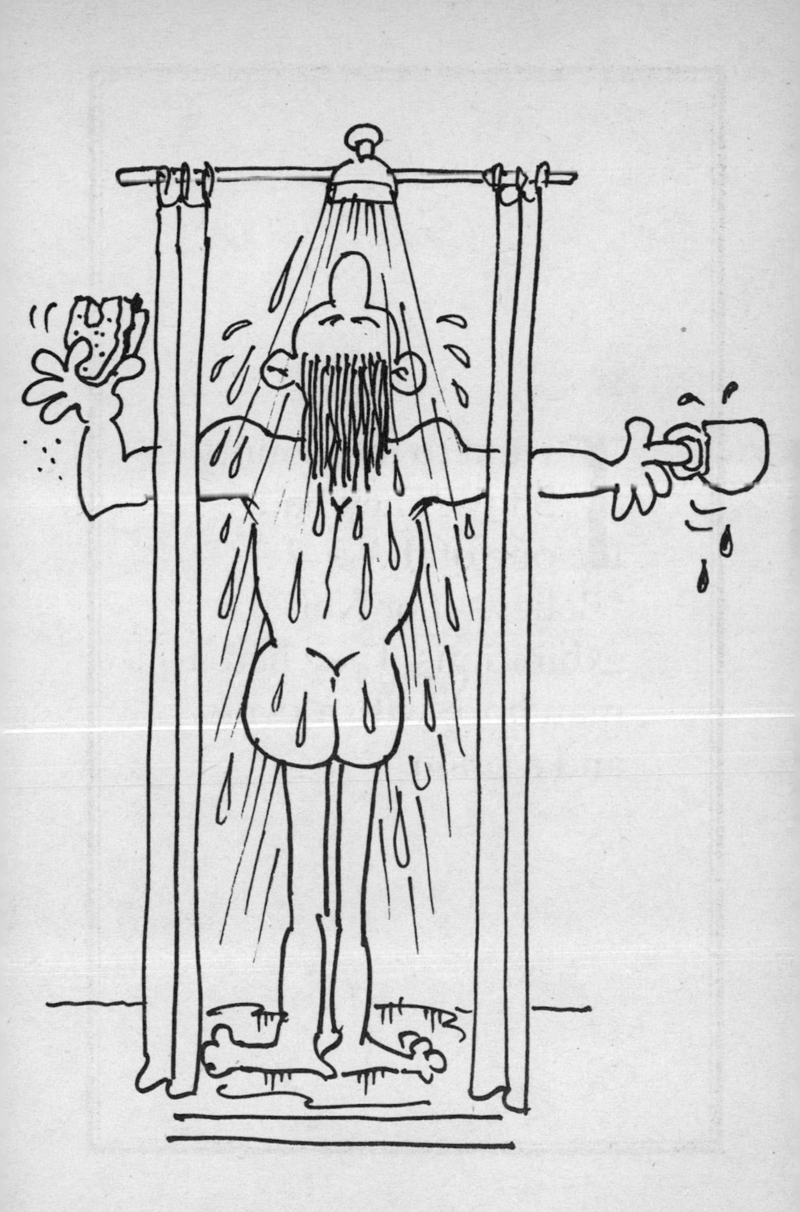

I went to the County Show. They had one of those "Believe It or Not" exhibitions. They had a man born with a penis and a brain.

Why did the stupid man put ice in his condom?

❦

To keep the swelling down.

What do you call a man with his hands handcuffed behind his back?

❦

Trustworthy.

If a man and woman jumped off a ten-storey building at the same time, which one would land first?

❦

The woman. The man would get lost.

What are two reasons why men don't mind their own business?

❦

1. No mind.
2. No business.

Why did the man pour beer into his waterbed?

❦

He wanted a foam mattress.

"Mummy, what happens when a car gets too old and rusty to work?" the little girl asked.

"Well," her mother said, "someone sells it to your father."

Why did the man ask all his friends to save their burned-out light bulbs?

❦

He needed them for the darkroom he was building.

What's the difference between a single 40-year-old woman and a single 40-year-old man?

❦

The 40-year-old woman thinks about having children and the 40-year-old man thinks about dating them.

Did you hear about the banker who's a great lover?

❦

He knows first-hand about the penalty for early withdrawal.

What did the experts of the nineties discover that could do the work of ten men?

❦

One woman.

Why is a man like a snowstorm?

❦

Because you don't know when he's coming, how many inches you'll get, or how long it'll stay.

What has an IQ of seven?

❦

Eight men.

Husband: Darling, if I died, would you get remarried?

Wife: I suppose so.

Husband: Would you sleep in the same bed?

Wife: He would be my husband, dear.

Husband: Would you give him my golf clubs?

Wife: No. He's left-handed.

Husband: Let's go out and have some fun tonight.

Wife: Okay, but if you get home before I do, just remember to leave the front door open.

The lovemaking was fast and furious. He was fast and she was furious.

Why did the man put two coins in his condom?

❦

Because if he can't come, he'll phone.

How can you tell if you're having a super orgasm?

❦

Your husband wakes up.

What do men and beer bottles have in common?

❦

They're both empty from the neck up.

Why are men like laxatives?

❦

They irritate the shit out of you.

The wife asked the husband why he was cutting a block of ice into little chunks. The husband said, "So they'll fit into the ice trays."

What do you call an intelligent man in England?

❦

A tourist.

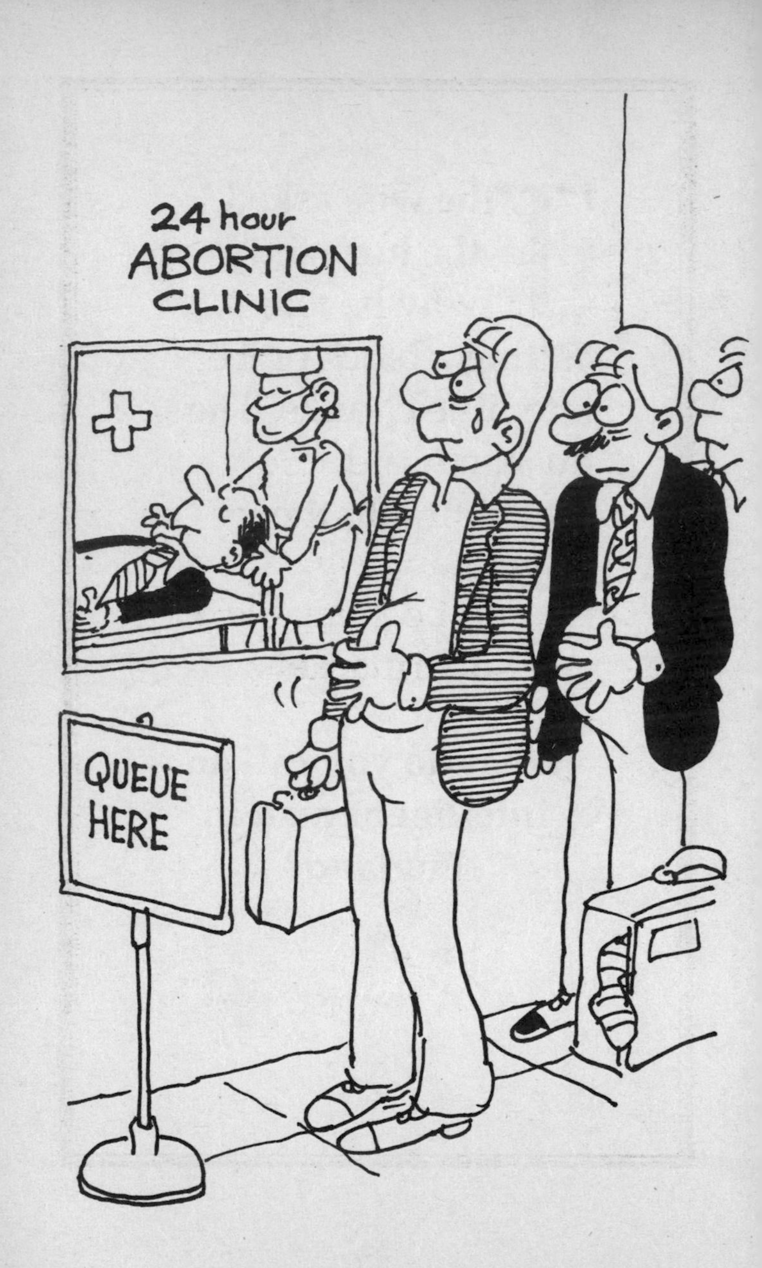
24 hour
ABORTION
CLINIC
QUEUE
HERE

If men got
pregnant...abortion
would be available at
supermarkets.

Why do footballers play on artificial turf?

❦

To keep them from grazing.

Wife: Darling, where do you want to go on holiday this year?

Husband: I want to go somewhere I've never been.

Wife: Well, how about the kitchen?

Did you hear about the man who lost his licence to practise medicine?

❦

He was caught having sex with some of his patients. It's such a shame. He was the best veterinarian in town.

Diamonds are a girl's best friend. Dogs are a man's best friend. Now you know which sex is smarter.

Why do many therapists charge men half price?

❦

They only have half a brain to analyse.

What is the definition of eternity?

❦

It's the length of time between when you come and when he leaves.

My marriage is childless - except for my husband.

A man is dating three women and wants to get married. He has to decide which one to ask. He gives them each £1,000. The first one spends £800 on clothes and puts the other £200 in the bank. The second one spends £200 on clothes and puts the other £800 in the bank. The third one puts the whole £1,000 in the bank. Which one does he marry?

The one with big breasts.

All men are created equal.

❦

Poor things.

What did the bride say on her wedding night?

❦

"I'm glad I didn't throw away my vibrator."

Nancy and Ronald Reagan go out to dinner. The waiter asks, "Ma'am, what would you like?"

Nancy answers, "Fillet of Sole, broiled no butter."

The waiter responds, "What about the vegetable?"

She answers, "He'll have the same thing."

Did you hear about the stupid man who...

Set the house on fire trying to light the radiator?

Studied for four days for his urine test?

Got stranded on the escalator during a power failure?

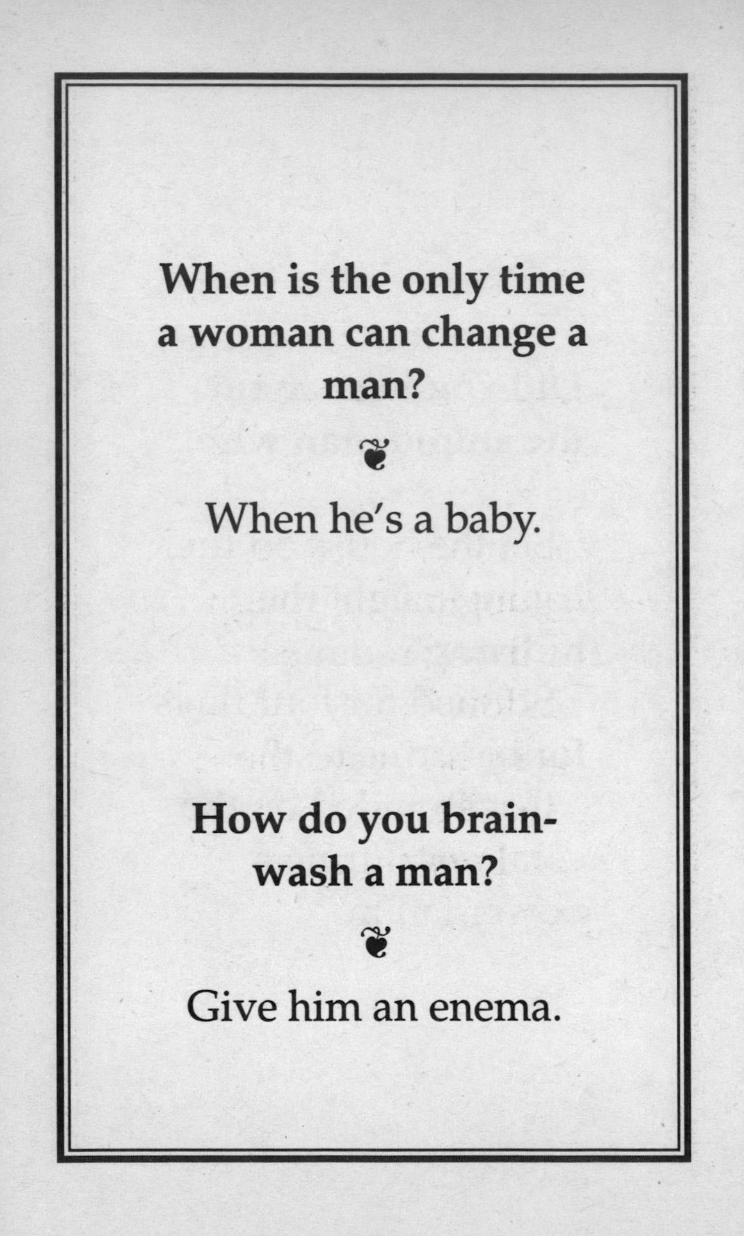

When is the only time a woman can change a man?

❦

When he's a baby.

How do you brain-wash a man?

❦

Give him an enema.

The neighbour said to the man. "You should close your curtains at night. Last night, I saw you and your wife making love through the living room window."

"Ha, ha," said the man. "The joke's on you. I wasn't even home!"

After their aerobics class, two women were changing in the locker room. One noticed that the other was putting on a pair of men's briefs.

"Hey," she said, "when did you start wearing men's underwear?" "Ever since my husband found them in my car," she replied.

Did you hear about the guy who wanted to go to the rock concert?

❦

The ticket prices were £17.50 in advance and £20.00 at the door. He decided not to go because he didn't want to pay £37.50.

How did the stupid man count the day's haul?

❦

"One fish...two fish...another fish...another fish...another fish."

Women who seek to be equal to men lack ambition.

A man came home and found his wife in bed with his best friend.

"What are you doing?" he shouted.

"See?" she said to her lover. "Didn't I tell you he was stupid?"

A stupid man picks up a woman in a bar and asks her to come to his apartment. She says, "I'd love to, but I have my menstrual cycle."

"Oh , that's okay," the man replies, "we can put it in the boot."

BAR
427

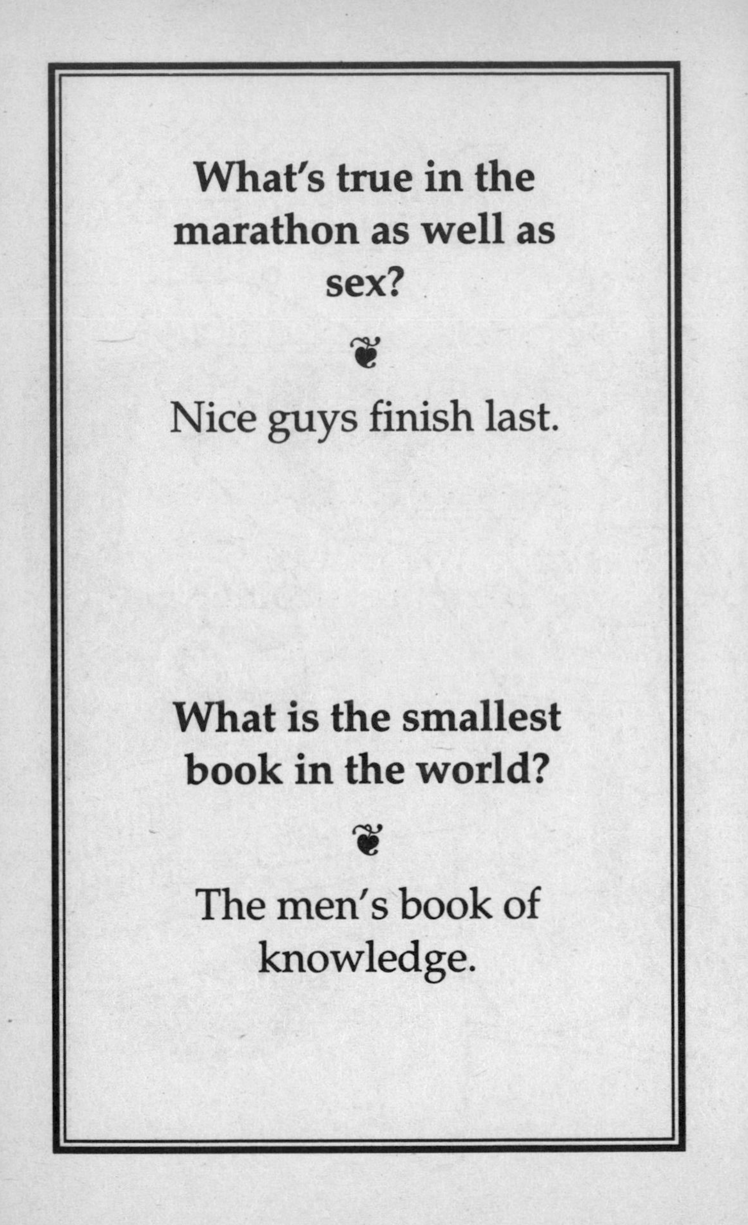

What's true in the marathon as well as sex?

❦

Nice guys finish last.

What is the smallest book in the world?

❦

The men's book of knowledge.

What do you call a man who supports a woman's career, helps prepare dinner, bathes the kids, and earns a six-figure income?

❦

Darling.

"Remember," the doctor told the couple, "no physical exertion for your husband. He's just had a major heart attack. And that includes sex. It could kill him."

That night, to avoid temptation, the man slept downstairs on the couch. But at three a.m. he woke up feeling horny and started for the stairs. Halfway up, he met his wife.

"I was just coming up the stairs to die."

"And I was just coming down the stairs to kill you."

What 's the difference between a stud and an average man?

❦

One's good for seconds, the other's good for seconds.

Why are all the dumb blonde jokes one-liners?

❦

So men can understand them.

Why do men name their penises?

❦

Because they want to be on first-name terms with the person who makes 95 per cent of their decisions.

A woman came into the police station to report her husband missing and described him as "29 years old, 6 feet, 3 inches tall, blonde, and handsome."

"I knew your husband," said the desk sergeant. "He was bald, fat and forty."

"I know," the woman said, "but who wants HIM back?"

Husband: Darling, I have some good news and some bad news. First, I've decided to run off with Elaine.

Wife: No kidding! What's the bad news?

What do men and decaffeinated coffee have in common?

❦

No active ingredients.

You don't need to lead a man into temptation - he can usually find it on his own.

What does a man call love?

❦

An erection.

There was a couple buying a new house from a builder. They walked through the house telling the contractor which colour to paint each room. Each time they told him a colour he would stick his head out the door and yell "Green side up!" After a while the couple asked if that was some kind of code for the colours they wanted. "No," said the contractor, "I have two guys outside laying the turf and I have to keep reminding them that the green side goes up."

What are a man's three favourite words to say to his woman?

❦

"While you're up..."

Did you hear about the man who won the gold medal at the Olympics?

❦

He had it bronzed.

How do men sort their laundry?

❦

"Filthy" and "Filthy but Wearable."

Why is it so hard for women to find men that are sensitive, caring, and good-looking?

❦

Because they already have boyfriends.

Most girls tend to marry men who are like their dads. This is the real reason mothers cry at weddings.

"Yesterday, I got a nice used car for my husband."

"I've seen your husband. It sounds like you got a good deal."

Why do men like masturbation?

❦

It's sex with the only one they really love.

My ex-husband converted me to religion.

❦

I never believed in hell till I married him.

Did you hear about the important businessman who refused to listen to his conscience?

❦

He didn't want to take advice from a total stranger.

Christopher Columbus set an example for men that has never been forgotten.

He didn't know where he was going, he didn't know where he was when he got there, and he did it on someone else's, namely a woman's, money.

The male executive didn't get to work until 11 a.m. His boss said, "You should have been here two hours ago."

The man replied, "Why, what happened?"

Husband: I don't know why you wear a bra. You've got nothing to put in it.

Wife: You wear pants, don't you?

What is gross stupidity?

❦

144 men in one room.

Sitting silently at the bar, the woman sipped her drink with an expression of extreme sadness on her face.

"Mary," asked a friend, "what in the world is the matter?"

"Oh, I'm having trouble with my husband," she explained.

"What happened?"

"Well, he told me he wasn't going to speak to me for thirty days."

"But ," her friend objected, "that ought to make you happy."

"It did, but today's the last day."

Lady in an antique shop: When I was here last week I saw a big mug with a flat head that holds a lot of beer. I'd like to buy it.

Antique dealer: I'm sorry, I can't sell it.

Lady: Why not?

Antique dealer: That's my husband.

What's the difference between a porcupine and a Porsche?

❦

A porcupine has pricks on the outside.

Adam asked Eve, "Do you still love me?" And Eve replied, "Who else?"

How many men does it take to screw in a light bulb?

❦

Just one. They'll screw anything.

How do most men define marriage?

❦

A very expensive way to get your laundry done free.

The man walked into the emergency room with both of his ears badly burnt. The man explained, "The phone rang and I picked up the iron by mistake."

The nurse asked, "How did you burn the other ear?"

"I did that," said the man, "when I went to phone the ambulance."

The man said to his therapist, "It first occurred to me that our marriage was in trouble when my wife won this all-expenses-paid trip for two to the Bahamas - and she went twice."

What are a stupid man's favourite pick-up lines?

1. Can I borrow ten pounds?

2. Is that your original nose?

3. Hi. I think your friend is really cute.

4. Can I talk to you? No? Then I guess sex is out of the question.

5. You have a little food stuck in your teeth.

6. Do you mind if I go on at great length about myself?

What is a man's view of safe sex?

❦

A padded headboard.

"Does your wife like to make love in the back seat of the car?"

"Yes...while I'm driving."

Why do men enjoy going to work?

❦

It's the only thing they can do for eight hours straight and still walk.

A telephone man was trying to measure the telephone pole but couldn't figure out how to climb up the pole. He radioed the office and they suggested that he lay the pole down on the ground and measure it. The phone man didn't like that idea.

"That won't work. I need to measure how high it is, not how long."

The hotel clerk told the businessman that there were no more rooms with a bath, and would he mind sharing a bath with another man.

"No," said the businessman, "not as long as he stays at his end of the bath."

Don't send a boy to do a man's job. Send a woman.

What do coffee, cats, and men have in common?

❦

They all keep you awake at night.

Did you hear about the stupid man who...

Thought "Twin Peaks" was about Dolly Parton?

Thinks belching is something to be proud of?

What's the difference between a man and a dog?

❦

A dog's more likely to come when you call.

The man started to become quite worried about his baldness. A friend recommended that he get a transplant. A month later he showed up with a heart on his head.

A man goes to have a little fun at a brothel that's located in a large building complex. Next door there's a pedicurist's office. He goes in there by mistake. The receptionist directs him to go on in and put "it" on the table. So he puts his penis on the table and waits. When the doctor comes in, she says, "Hey, that's not a foot." And the man replies, "So, what's a couple of inches more or less?"

What's the difference between a man and a savings account?

❦

A savings account pays at least a little interest to you.

Only a man would buy a £500 car and put a £4,000 stereo in it.

Why did the expectant father want to name his baby Oscar?

❦

Because it was his best performance all year.

What's the difference between men and Halley's Comet?

❦

Halley's Comet is predictable.

One friend said to the other, "So, does your wife have orgasms?"

"Well, she says she does. I've never been there when it happened though."

Why do most men lead a dog's life?

❦

It's a very similar existence. They both come in with muddy feet, make themselves comfortable by the fire and wait to be fed.

How does the typical man dust?

❦

He sprays Pledge in the air and just hopes that it lands on the right pieces of furniture.

Why did God create man?

❦

Because a vibrator can't mow the lawn.

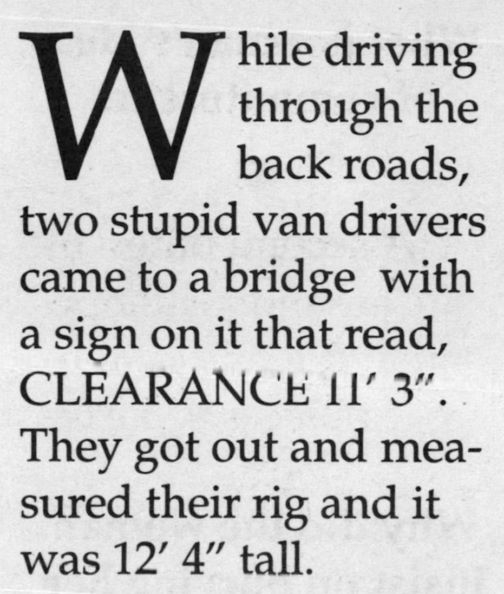

While driving through the back roads, two stupid van drivers came to a bridge with a sign on it that read, CLEARANCE 11′ 3″. They got out and measured their rig and it was 12′ 4″ tall.

"What do you think?" said one to the other.

The driver looked around and replied, "Not a policeman in sight. Let's take a chance."

What is a man's idea of commitment?

❦

A second date.

Why did the woman insist on burying her husband 12 feet under?

❦

Because deep down, he was a good person.

I married beneath me.
Most women do.

Why were men given larger brains than dogs?

❦

So they wouldn't hump women's legs at cocktail parties.

Did you hear about the guy who was so stupid he couldn't spell BMW?

Two guys were strolling down the street when one guy exclaimed, "How sad - a dead bird."

The other looked up and said, "Where?"

A man walks into a bar and sees a moose head on the wall. He asks the barman if it would be all right to go into the next room to see the rest of it.

Was that man lazy! Every night he would sit for hours in front of the TV... sometimes he even turned it on.

Why did the man buy a new car?

❦

He couldn't keep up the payments on the old one.

A stupid man goes to the travel agency and says, "I'd like a round-trip ticket, please."

"Where to?" the agent asks.

"Why, back here, of course."

Two men were passengers on a four-engine plane. Suddenly, one engine failed and the pilot announced that the plane would now be fifteen minutes late. A short time later another engine failed. The pilot announced they would be thirty minutes late. Then the third engine failed and the pilot announced that they would be one hour late. At this point, one man said to the other, " If the fourth engine quits, we could be up here all day."

Give a man a fish and you feed him for a day. Teach a man to fish, and you get rid of him at weekends.

Did you hear about the stupid guy who walked into a shop selling telephones?

❦

He bought a cordless phone for every room in the house.

A man walks by the police station and sees a sign that says, "Man wanted for Bank Robbery." So he goes inside and applies for the job.

I took him for better or worse, but he's worse than I took him for.

A woman calls her husband at home. "I won the Pools. Two million pounds. Start packing."

"What should I pack? Where are we going?" he replies.

"I don't care," says the wife. "Just be out of the house by the time I get home."

A pompous man asked a woman, "Why do you suppose it is that women so utterly lack a sense of humour?"

"God did it on purpose," she replied, "so that we may love men instead of laugh at them."

Husband to Wife: Do you ever look at a man and wish you were single again?

Wife: Yes, every morning

My therapist told me to use some imagination while making love with my husband.

I said, "You mean imagine it's good?"

Why did the man walk around with his flies open?

❦

Just in case he had to count to eleven.

Why don't men like pickles?

❦

They keep getting their heads stuck in the jar.

Did you hear about the man who died from jumping out of an aeroplane?

❦

It seems he was watching the movie, forgot where he was and stepped out for some popcorn.

Why do men have such flat foreheads and receding hair-lines?

❦

Every time they don't know the answer to a question, they hit themselves on the fore-head.

Did you hear about the man who bought an A.M. radio?

❦

It took him months before he realized he could play it at night, too.

Did you hear about the stupid man who bought a car bra so his headlights wouldn't sag?

Did you hear about the man who bought a rowing machine but returned it to the store?

❦

He said it wouldn't fit in the bathtub.

Definition of an immature, macho man: One that uses "Magnum" extra-large condoms for his water bombs.

The only time a man will watch "Oprah" is when the show is on "female nymphos and where they hang out."

Did you hear about the guy who went to Weight Watchers and lost 30 lbs of ugly fat?

❦

He found out he was still ugly.

What's the greatest mystery about men?

❦

How they can get older but still manage to remain immature.

Scene at a singles bar:

Man: How would you like to follow me back to my place?

Woman: Can two people fit under a rock?

What quality do most men look for in a woman?

❦

Breathing.

There is a method of male birth control.

❦

It's called their personality.

Did you hear about the man who was stabbed 20 times in the head?

❦

He was trying to eat with a fork.

A football fan lost a £50 bet on a TV football play.

❦

He lost another £50 on the instant replay.

Why did the man drive around the block 42 times?

❦

His indicator was stuck.

What happened to two men who jumped out of a plane without parachutes?

❦

Who cares?

What do you call it when a bunch of guys go swimming?

❦

A Bay of Pigs.

Why do men look forward to family reunions?

❦

They see it as a great way to meet women.

Mummy, what does "humour him" mean?

❦

You'll have to wait until you're married to find that one out, dear.

Two middle-aged women discussing husbands:

1st woman: Does your husband still look at younger women?

2nd woman: Yes, but he can't remember why.

What do men call a man who can cook?

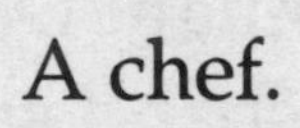

A chef.

What do men call a woman who can cook?

A housewife.

"Is your husband loving and caring?"

"Oh yes, he replaces the batteries in my vibrator once a month."

What does a stupid man do when he wants to impress a new girlfriend?

❦

Show her how quickly he can come.

When do you know a man is definitely lying?

❦

When he keeps saying "BELIEVE ME."

What does a stupid man do when confronted by a toddler having a tantrum?

❦

Stamp his feet and shout for mother.

How can you tell if a man is dead?

❦

He stays stiff for more than 2 minutes.

What invention cut the average man's daily workload by 50 per cent?

❦

The self-winding watch.

What's a man's idea of helping with the housework?

❦

Lifting his legs so you can vacuum.

Why is your husband like your period?

❦

He only comes once a month.

Is your husband good at foreplay?

❦

You must be joking, he thinks cunnilingus is an Irish airline.

Why do men drive fast, flashy cars?

❦

Because they can't get road tax for their penises.

How can you tell if a man's done the washing?

❦

All your clothes are now that fashionable grey colour.

Why would you want to share your house with a man?

❦

The landlord won't let you keep a cat.

Why are men better than cats?

❦

Men only piss on the carpet in the bathroom.

Why would you employ a man?

❦

Because no women applied and there's a shortage of fish on the job market

What do toilets and anniversaries have in common?

❦

Men always miss them.

Do you know any stupid men jokes?

If so, please send them to:

Stupid Men Jokes
Michael O'Mara Books
9 Lion Yard
Tremadoc Road
Clapham
London SW4 7NQ

Sorry, no credit or remuneration can be given, but the great ones will be considered for the second volume, and we do want to hear from you.

ABOUT THE AUTHOR

Nancy Gray is a full-time professional comedian who manages to pack a feminist wallop into a joke and still leave both sexes doubled over in laughter. These days, she's everywhere - on the road for forty-four weeks last year, she has appeared in over 200 cities since 1990. Calling herself a "PG-13" version of *Good Housekeeping*, she has made several appearances on the Comedy Channel, was invited to perform at "Comic Relief" three years in a row, and has opened for the likes of Howie Mandel, Pat Paulson, and Rich Hall. Nancy currently lives in Charlotte, North Carolina.